Exam Dumps

PSM Professional Scrum Master I Exam Prep and Dumps

SCRUM PSM I Exam Guidebook
Updated questions

Welcome to Byte Books: Your Path to Exam Success!

At Byte Books, we are dedicated to helping aspiring professionals achieve their career goals through comprehensive exam certification guides and practice questions. We understand that exams can be daunting, and the path to success may seem challenging. That's why we're here to provide you with the knowledge, confidence, and support you need to excel in your chosen field.

Our Mission: Empowering Your Success

Our mission is simple yet powerful: to empower your success. We believe that with the right study materials and guidance, you can overcome any exam hurdle and unlock new opportunities for personal and professional growth. At Byte Books, we go the extra mile to curate top-notch resources that cater to a wide range of certification exams, covering various industries and professions.

QUESTION 1

When many Scrum Teams are working on the same product, should all of their Increments be integrated every Sprint?

A. Yes, but only for Scrum Teams whose work has dependencies.
B. Yes, otherwise the Product Owners (and stakeholders) may not be able to accurately inspect what is done.
C. No, each Scrum Team stands alone.
D. No, that is far too hard and must be done in a hardening Sprint.

QUESTION 2

Scrum has a role called "Project Manager".

A. True
B. False

QUESTION 3

Which answer best describes the topics covered in Sprint Planning?

A. What to do and who will do it.
B. How conditions have changed and how the Product Backlog should evolve.
C. What can be done and how to do it.
D. What went wrong in the last Sprint and what to do differently this Sprint.
E. Who is on the team and what team member roles will be.

QUESTION 4

Who determines when it is appropriate to update the Sprint Backlog during a Sprint?

A. The Project Manager.
B. The Development Team.
C. The Scrum Team.
D. The Product Owner.

QUESTION 5

When do Development Team members take ownership of a Sprint Backlog item? (Choose the best answer.)

A. At the Sprint planning meeting.
B. During the Daily Scrum.
C. Never. All Sprint Backlog Items are "owned" by the entire Scrum Team.
D. Whenever a team member can accommodate more work.

QUESTION 6

The purpose of a Sprint is to produce a done Increment of product.

A. True
B. False

QUESTION 7

Five new Scrum Teams have been created to build one product. A few of the developers on one of the Development Teams ask the Scrum Master how to coordinate their work with the order teams. What should the Scrum Master do?

A. Teach the Product Owner to work with the lead developers on ordering Product Backlog in a way to avoid too much technical and development overlap during a Sprint.
B. Teach them that it is their responsibility to work with the other teams to create an integrated Increment.
C. Collect the Sprint tasks from the teams at the end of their Sprint Planning and merge that into a consolidated plan for the entire Sprint.
D. Visit the five teams each day to inspect that their Sprint Backlogs are aligned.

QUESTION 8

Which two things should the Development Team do during the first Sprint? (Choose two.)

A. Make up a plan for the rest of the project.
B. Analyze, describe, and document the requirements for the subsequent Sprints.
C. Develop at least one piece of functionality.
D. Analyze, design, and describe the complete architecture and infrastructure.
E. Create an increment of potentially releasable software.

QUESTION 9

What are three ways Scrum promotes self-organization? (Choose three.)

A. By not allowing documentation.
B. By the Development Team deciding what work to do in a Sprint.
C. By preventing stakeholders from entering the development room.
D. By removing titles for Development Team members.
E. By being a lightweight framework.

QUESTION 10

What is the key concern when multiple Development Teams are working from the same Product Backlog?

A. Minimizing dependencies between teams.
B. Clear definition of requirements.
C. Meeting original scope projections.
D. Making sure there's enough work for everyone on every team.
E. Maximizing velocity.

QUESTION 11

The Product Owner must release each Increment to production.

A. When it makes sense.
B. To make sure the Development Team is done every Sprint.
C. Whenever the product is free of defects.
D. Without exception.

QUESTION 12

A properly functioning Scrum Team will have at least one Release Sprint and may well have several.

A. True
B. False

QUESTION 13

Scrum is a methodology that tells in detail how to build software incrementally.

A. True
B. False

QUESTION 14

As the Sprint Planning meeting progresses, the Development Team sees that the workload is greater than they can handle. Which two are valid actions? (Choose two.)

A. Recruit additional Development Team members before the work can begin.
B. The Development Team ensures that the Product Owner is aware, starts the Sprint, and monitors progress.
C. Cancel the Sprint.
D. Remove or change selected Product Backlog items.
E. The Development Team works overtime during this Sprint.

QUESTION 15

During a Sprint, when is new work or further decomposition of work added to the Sprint Backlog?

A. When the Product Owner identifies new work.
B. As soon as possible after they are identified.
C. When the Scrum Master has time to enter them.
D. During the Daily Scrum after the Development Team approves them.

QUESTION 16

What is the main reason for the Scrum Master to be at the Daily Scrum?

A. To gather status and progress information to report to management.
B. To write down any changes to the Sprint Backlog, including adding new items, and tracking progress on the burn-down.
C. He or she does not have to be there; he or she only has to ensure the Development Team has a Daily Scrum.
D. To make sure every team member answers the three questions.

QUESTION 17

You have six teams using a traditional method to deliver a product. Your management has asked you to start using Scrum. In the initial project there were separate plans and teams for the layers of a software system, i.e. one for the front-end, one for the middle tier, one for the back-end, and one for the interfaces and services. This resembles what is known as component teams. But you have read that it's a good idea to have teams organized by feature.

What are the advantages of keeping component teams while starting Scrum?

A. There's less initial disruption than organizing into new teams. As they start, they will discover what works best, and how to potentially re-organize towards this.
B. Component teams generally have the skills needed to create a working Increment of software that provides business value.
C. Because they have worked together for some time, they are likely able to start producing shippable Increments faster that new feature teams would.
D. There are fewer cross-team dependencies than working in feature teams.

QUESTION 18

How should Product Backlog items be chosen when multiple Scrum Teams work from the same Product Backlog?

A. The Scrum Team with the highest velocity pulls Product Backlog items first.
B. The Development Teams pull in work in agreement with the Product Owner.
C. The Product Owner should provide each team with its own Product Backlog.
D. Each Scrum Team takes an equal numbers of items.
E. The Product Owner decides.

QUESTION 19

How often should Scrum Team membership change?

A. As needed, while taking into account a short term reduction in productivity.
B. Never, because it reduces productivity.
C. As needed, with no special allowance for changes in productivity.
D. Every Sprint to promote shared learning.

QUESTION 20

Who should make sure everyone on the Development Team does his or her tasks for the Sprint?

A. The Project Manager.
B. The Product Owner.
C. The Scrum Master.
D. The Development Team.
E. All of the above.

QUESTION 21

Which statement best describes Scrum?

A. A defined and predictive process that conforms to the principles of Scientific Management.
B. A complete methodology that defines how to develop software.
C. A cookbook that defines best practices for software development.
D. A framework within which complex products in complex environments are developed.

QUESTION 22
Who starts the Daily Scrum?

A. The person coming in last. This encourages people to be on time and helps to stay within the time-box.
B. Whoever the Development Team decides should start.
C. The person who has the token.
D. The Scrum Master. This ensures that the Development Team has the meeting and stays within the time-box.
E. The person who last broke the build.

QUESTION 23
A Development Team selects a set of Product Backlog items for a Sprint Backlog with the intent to get the selected items "Done" by the end of the Sprint. Which three phrases best describe the purpose of a definition of "Done"? (Choose three.)

A. It controls whether the developers have performed their tasks.
B. It provides a template for elements that need to be included in the technical documentation.
C. It creates transparency over the work inspected at the Sprint Review.
D. It trucks the percent completeness of a Product Backlog item.
E. It guides the Development Team is creating a forecast at the Sprint Planning.
F. It defines what it takes for an Increment to be ready for release.

QUESTION 24
Select two ways in which technical debt impacts transparency. (Choose two.)

A. When calculated and estimated, the total amount of technical debt shows exactly how long until the Product Owner can release the Increment.
B. It leads to false assumptions about the current state of the system, specifically of an Increment being releasable at the end of a Sprint.
C. As development progresses and code is added, the system becomes more difficult to stabilize, which results in future work being slowed down in unpredictable ways.
D. It enhances transparency for the Product Owner as a Development Team is not allowed to do additional feature development in a Sprint as long as there is technical debt.

QUESTION 25

Which of these may a Development Team deliver at the end of a Sprint?

A. Failing unit tests, to identify acceptance tests for the next Sprint.
B. An increment of software with minor known bugs in it.
C. An increment of working software that is "done".
D. A single document, if that is what the Scrum Master asked for.

QUESTION 26

Who is responsible for managing the progress of work during a Sprint?

A. The Scrum Master.
B. The Development Team.
C. The Product Owner.
D. The most junior member of the Team.

QUESTION 27

Which of the following are true about the length of the Sprint? (Choose two.)

A. The length of the Sprint should be proportional to the work that is done in between Sprints.
B. It is best to have Sprints of consistent length throughout a development effort.
C. Sprint length is determined during Sprint Planning, and should hold the time it will take to code the planned features in the upcoming Sprint, but does not include time for any testing.
D. Sprint length is determined during Sprint Planning, and should be long enough to make sure the Development Team can deliver what is to be accomplished in the upcoming Sprint.
E. All Sprints must be 1 month or less.

QUESTION 28

The CEO asks the Development Team to add a "very important" item to a Sprint that is in progress. What should the Development Team do?

A. Add the item to the current Sprint and drop an item of equal size.
B. Add the item to the current Sprint without any adjustments.
C. Inform the Product Owner so he/she can work with the CEO.
D. Add the item to the next Sprint.

QUESTION 29

What is the role of management in Scrum? (Choose the best answer.)

A. To present the Scrum Teams with insights and resources that help them improve.
B. To monitor the Development Team's productivity.
C. To identify and remove people that aren't working hard enough.
D. To continually monitor staffing levels of the Scrum Team.

QUESTION 30

Which technique is the best way the Scrum Master can ensure that the Development Team communicates effectively with the Product Owner?

A. Monitor communications between them and facilitate direct collaboration.
B. Teach the Development Team to talk in terms of business needs and objectives.
C. Teach the Product Owner about the technologies employed during the Sprints.
D. Act as a go-between for them.

QUESTION 31

The length of a Sprint should be:

A. Short enough to keep the business risk acceptable to the Product Owner.

B. Short enough to be able to synchronize the development work with other business events.

C. No more than one calendar month.

D. All of these answers are correct.

QUESTION 32

During a Sprint Retrospective, for what is the Product Owner responsible?

A. Participating as a Scrum Team member.

B. Summarizing and reporting the discussions to the stakeholders that he/she represents in the Scrum Team.

C. Capturing requirements for the Product Backlog.

D. The Product Owner should not take part in Sprint Retrospectives.

QUESTION 33

Marian is the Product Owner envisioning a project for a new release of her product. She made a projection of a release date based upon a sustained velocity of 17 completed units of work per Sprint. Over the first 3 Sprints, the average velocity was 13 for work that the Development Team estimated as 90% done. The Development Teams, feeling the need to meet the plan, figured that a velocity of 17 was within their reach.

A good way to continue is:

A. The Development Team makes sure that all of the selected scope per Sprint is as "Done" as possible. The undone work is estimated and added to the Sprint Backlog of the next Sprint, so it doesn't mess up the Product Backlog.

B. Add enough people to the Development Team for the deadline to be made.

C. The opportunity to inspect and adapt is lost. Opaqueness has replaced transparency. Predictability has dropped below zero. The produced software is not usable. As the rules of Scrum have not been respected, it is the Scrum Master's duty to assess whether repair is possible, or a restart with a more reliable team. If not, the Scrum Master should cancel the project.

D. The Development Team should remind Marian to find funding for enough Release Sprints in which the remaining work can be done.

QUESTION 34

The Product Owner is not collaborating with the Development Team during the Sprint. What are two valuable actions for a Scrum Master to take? (Choose two.)

A. Inform the Product Owner's functional manager.
B. Stop the Sprint, send the Product Owner to a course and restart.
C. Bring up the problem in the Sprint Retrospective.
D. Coach the Product Owner in the values of Scrum and incremental delivery.
E. Nominate a proxy Product Owner.

QUESTION 35

Multiple Scrum Teams working on the same product or system all select work from the same Product Backlog.

A. True
B. False

QUESTION 36

Multiple Scrum Teams working on the same project must have the same Sprint start date.

A. True
B. False

QUESTION 37
A Product Owner wants advice from the Scrum Master about estimating work in Scrum. Which of these is the guideline that a Scrum Master should give?

A. Product Backlog items must be estimated in story points.
B. Estimates are made by the Development Team.
C. Estimates must be in relative units.
D. Scrum forbids estimating.
E. Estimates are made by the Product Owner, but are best checked with the Development Team.

QUESTION 38

What is the time-box for the Sprint Planning meeting?

A. 4 Hours for a monthly Sprint.
B. 8 Hours for a monthly Sprint.

C. Monthly.
D. Whenever it is done.

QUESTION 39

A Scrum Master is keeping a list of open impediments, but it is growing and he/she has been able to resolve only a small portion of the impediments. Which three techniques would be most helpful in this situation? (Choose three.)

A. Consulting with the Development Team.
B. Prioritizing the list and working on them in order.
C. Arranging a triage meeting with all project managers.
D. Alerting management to the impediments and their impact.

QUESTION 40

A product Increment must be released to production at the end of each Sprint.

A. True
B. False

QUESTION 41

How is management external to the Scrum Team involved in the Daily Scrum?

A. The Scrum Master speaks on their behalf.
B. The Development Team self-manages and is the only management required at the Daily Scrum.
C. Management gives an update at the start of each Daily Scrum.
D. The Product Owner represents their opinions.

QUESTION 42

To get started in terms of what to build, Scrum requires no more than a Product Owner with enough ideas for a first Sprint, a Development Team to implement those ideas and a Scrum Master to help guide the process.

A. True
B. False

QUESTION 43

What is the time-box for the Sprint Review?

A. As long as needed.
B. 2 hours for a monthly Sprint.
C. 4 hours for a monthly Sprint.
D. 4 hours and longer as needed.
E. 1 day

QUESTION 44

What is the tactic a Scrum Master should use to divide a group of 100 people into multiple Development Teams?

A. Create teams based on their skills across multiple layers (such as database, UI, etc.)
B. Ask the Product Owner to assign the people to teams.
C. Ask the developers to divide themselves into teams.

QUESTION 45

The Sprint Review is mainly an inspect and adapt opportunity for which group?

A. The Development Team and stakeholders.
B. The Product Owner and Development Team.
C. The Scrum Team and stakeholders.
D. The Product Owner and management.
E. The Development Team and management.
F. The Product Owner and stakeholders.

QUESTION 46

Which of the following best describes an increment of working software?

A. A decomposition of all Product Backlog items into tasks for future Sprint Backlog lists.
B. Additional features in a usable state that complement those delivered in previous iterations.
C. A new user interface design for functionality delivered in previous iterations.
D. An automated test suite to verify functionality delivered in previous iterations.
E. UML diagrams that describe how to deliver functionality in future iterations.

QUESTION 47

The Product Owner determines how many Product Backlog items the Development Team selects for a Sprint.

A. False.
B. True, accordingly to what was committed to the stakeholders.
C. True, but only after confirmation by the resource manager that the Team has enough capacity.
D. True.
E. False, the Scrum Master does that.
F. False, capacity and commitment are the Project manager's responsibility.

QUESTION 48

Which three of the following are feedback loops in Scrum? (Choose three.)

A. Sprint Review.
B. Release Planning.
C. Sprint Retrospective.
D. Refinement Meeting.
E. Daily Scrum.

QUESTION 49

When is the Sprint Backlog created?

A. At the beginning of the project.
B. During the Sprint Planning meeting.
C. Prior to the Sprint Planning meeting.
D. During the Sprint.

QUESTION 50

Which of the following services are appropriate for a Scrum Master in regard to the Daily Scrum?

A. Lead the discussions of the Development Team.
B. Make sure that all 3 questions have been answered by each member of the team.
C. Keep track of whether each team member has a chance to speak.
D. Teach the Development Team to keep the Daily Scrum within the 15 minute time-box.
E. All of the above.

QUESTION 51

What are the two primary ways a Scrum Master keeps a Development Team working at its highest level of productivity? (Choose two.)

A. By ensuring the meetings start and end at the proper time.
B. By removing impediments that hinder the Development Team.
C. By facilitating Development Team decisions.
D. By keeping high value features high in the Product Backlog.

QUESTION 52

Cross-functional teams are optimized to work on one technical layer of a system only (e.g. GUI, database, middle tier, interfaces).

A. True
B. False

QUESTION 53

A Scrum Master is working with a Development Team that has members in different physical locations. The Development Team meets in a variety of meeting rooms and has much to do logistically (for example, set up conference calls) before the Daily Scrum. What action should the Scrum Master take?

A. Allow the Development Team to self-manage and determine for itself what to do.
B. Set up the meeting and tell the Development Team that is how it will be done.
C. Ask the Development Team members to alternate who is responsible for meeting setup.
D. Inform management and ask them to solve it.

QUESTION 54

Who can abnormally terminate a Sprint?

A. The Scrum Master
B. The Development Team or its members.
C. The Product Owner
D. The Stakeholders

QUESTION 55

The Sprint Goal is a result of Sprint Planning, as is the Sprint Backlog.

A. True
B. False

QUESTION 56

When should a Sprint Goal be created?

A. It should have been created in the previous Sprint during Product Backlog refinement.
B. It must be established before Sprint Planning in order to begin planning.
C. A Sprint Goal is not mandatory in Scrum.
D. At any time during the Sprint.
E. During Sprint Planning.

QUESTION 57

During a Sprint Retrospective, the Development Team proposes moving the Daily Scrum to only occur on Tuesdays and Thursdays. Which two are the most appropriate responses for the Scrum Master? (Choose two.)

A. Consider the request and decide on which days the Daily Scrum should occur.
B. Coach the team on why the Daily Scrum is important as an opportunity to update the plan.
C. Have the developers vote.
D. Learn why the Development Team wants this and work with them to improve the outcome of the Daily Scrum.
E. Acknowledge and support the self-organizing team's decision.

QUESTION 58

As the Development Team starts work during the Sprint, it realizes it has selected too much work to finish in the Sprint. What should it do?

A. Inform the Product Owner at the Sprint Review, but prior to the demonstration.
B. Find another Scrum Team to give the excess work to.
C. As soon as possible in the Sprint, work with the Product Owner to remove some work or Product Backlog items.
D. Reduce the definition of "Done" and get all of the Product Backlog items "Done" by the new definition.

QUESTION 59

In accordance with Scrum theory, how should a group of 100 people be divided into multiple Development Teams?

A. Understanding the product, the product vision and the rules of the Scrum framework, the group divides itself into teams.
B. It doesn't really matter because you can rotate the teams every Sprint to spread knowledge.
C. Check with the allocation department to see who has worked together before and make these the first teams.
D. Create a matrix of skills, seniority, and level of experience to assign people to teams.

QUESTION 60
A new developer is having continuing conflicts with existing Development Team members and creating a hostile environment. If necessary, who is responsible for removing the team member?

A. The hiring manager is responsible, because he/she hired the developer.
B. The Scrum Manager is responsible, because he/she removes Impediments.
C. The Development Team is responsible, and may need help from the Scrum Master.
D. The Product Owner is responsible, because he/she controls the return on investment (ROI).

QUESTION 61

Which statement best describes the Sprint Review?

A. It is used to congratulate the Development Team if it did what it forecast, or to punish the Development Team if it failed to meet its forecast.
B. It is a demo at the end of the Sprint for everyone in the organization to check on the work done.
C. It is a mechanism to control the Development Team's activities during a Sprint.
D. It is when the Scrum Team and stakeholders inspect the outcome of a Sprint and figure out what to do next.

QUESTION 62

Who owns the Sprint Backlog?

A. The Scrum Team.
B. The Product Owner.
C. The Scrum Master.
D. The Development Team.

QUESTION 63

When might a Sprint be abnormally cancelled?

A. When the Development Team feels that the work is too hard.
B. When the Sprint Goal becomes obsolete.
C. When the sales department has an important new opportunity.
D. When it becomes clear that not everything will be finished by the end of the Sprint.

QUESTION 64

Why does the Product Owner want the Development Team to adhere to its definition of "Done"?

A. To have complete transparency into what has been done at the end of each Sprint.
B. To be able to reprimand the team when they don't meet their velocity goal for the Sprint.
C. To know what the team will deliver over the next three Sprints.
D. To predict the team's productivity over time.

QUESTION 65

During a Sprint Retrospective, for what is the Scrum Master responsible?

A. Prioritizing the resulting action items.
B. Participating as a Scrum team member and facilitating as requested or needed.
C. Acting as a scribe to capture the Development Team's answers.
D. Summarizing and reporting the discussions to management.

QUESTION 66

The Development Team should have all the skills needed to:

A. Turn Product Backlog items into an Increment of potentially releasable product functionality.
B. Do all of the development work, except for specialized testing that requires additional tools and environments.
C. Complete the project within the date and cost as calculated by the Product Owner.

QUESTION 67

The Scrum Master observes the Product Owner struggling with ordering the Product Backlog. What is an appropriate action for the Scrum Master to take?

A. Suggest the Product Owner extend the Sprint, so he can have more time to order the Product Backlog.
B. Suggest that the Development Team does the ordering to be sure that it is a feasible ordering of work.
C. Offer the Product Owner help in understanding that the goal of ordering the Product Backlog is to maximize value.
D. Present the Product Owner with an ordered Product Backlog to use.
E. Encourage the Product Owner to work with the Development Team to see which items technically are fastest to implement.

QUESTION 68

Choose two responsibilities of a self-organizing Development Team. (Choose two.)

A. Reorder the Product Backlog.
B. Pull Product Backlog items for the Sprint.
C. Do the work planned in the Sprint Backlog.
D. Increase velocity.
E. Report daily progress to stakeholders.

QUESTION 69

If two Scrum Teams are added to the development of a product that previously had only one Scrum Team, what will be the immediate impact on the productivity of the original Scrum Team? (Choose the best answer.)

A. Its productivity is likely to decrease.
B. Its productivity is likely to stay the same.
C. Its productivity is likely to increase.
D. We do not know until a Sprint has run.

QUESTION 70

A Scrum Master is introducing Scrum to a new Development Team. The Development Team has decided that a Sprint Retrospective is unnecessary. What action should the Scrum Master take?

A. Call a meeting between the Development Team and senior management.
B. Comply with the decision of the self-organizing team.
C. Consult with the Product Owner to see how he/she feels about the situation.
D. Begin facilitating productive and useful Sprint Retrospectives.

QUESTION 71

Which of the following are true about the Product Owner role? (Choose two.)

A. The Product Owner is one person.
B. The Product Owner is accountable for ordering the Product Backlog.
C. Multiple people can share the Product Owner role on a Scrum Team.
D. The Product Owner role can be played by a committee or a team of people.

QUESTION 72

When does the second Sprint start?

A. Once the architectural changes for the second Sprint have been approved by the senior architect.
B. After the Product Backlog for the second Sprint has been selected.
C. Immediately after the first Sprint.
D. After the customer completes acceptance testing of the first Sprint.

QUESTION 73

What is included in the Sprint Backlog?

A. User Stories.
B. Tasks.
C. Use Cases.
D. Tests.
E. Any of the above (or others) which are a decomposition of the selected Product Backlog items.

QUESTION 74

Who determines how work is performed during the Sprint?

A. Architects.

B. The Development Team.
C. The Scrum Master.
D. Subject matter experts.
E. Development Team managers.

QUESTION 75

Why should the Product Owner be present at the Daily Scrum?

A. He/She doesn't need to be there.
B. To hear about impediments in functionality.
C. To represent the stakeholders' point of view.
D. To participate as a Scrum Team member.

QUESTION 76

Who is responsible for clearly expressing Product Backlog items?

A. The Scrum Master, or the Scrum Master may have the Development Team do it.
B. The Scrum Master.
C. The Product Owner.
D. The business analyst who represents the Product Owner in the Development Team.

QUESTION 77

At the end of a Sprint Product Backlog item worked on during the Sprint does not meet the definition of "Done". What two things should happen with the undone Product Backlog item? (Choose two.)

A. If the stakeholders agree, the Product Owner can accept it and release it to the users.
B. Put it on the Product Backlog for the Product Owner to decide what to do with it.
C. Review the item, add the "Done" part of the estimate to the velocity and create a Story for the remaining work.
D. Do not include the item in the Increment this Sprint.

QUESTION 78

If burndown charts are used to visualize progress, what does a trend line through a release burndown chart indicate?

A. The evolution of the cost spent on the project.
B. When all work will be completed to the Scrum Team can be released for other work.
C. When the work remaining will likely be completed if nothing changes on the Product Backlog or the Development Team.
D. When the project will be over if the Product Owner removes work that is equal in effort to any new work that is added.

QUESTION 79

Who is responsible for engaging the stakeholders?

A. The Business Analyst.
B. The Development Team.
C. The Team Manager.
D. The Project Manager.
E. The Product Owner.

QUESTION 80

How much work must a Development Team do to a Product Backlog
item it selects for a Sprint?

A. A proportional amount of time on analysis, design, programming,
   testing, and documentation.
B. As much as it can fit into the Sprint. Any remaining work will be
   transferred to a subsequent Sprint.
C. All development work and at least some testing.
D. As much as it has told the Product Owner will be done for every
   Product Backlog item it selects in conformance with the definition of
   "Done".

QUESTION 81

Which statement best describes the Sprint Backlog as outcome of the
Sprint Planning?

A. It is a complete list of all work to be done in a Sprint.
B. Every item has a designated owner.
C. Each task is estimated in hours.
D. It is the Development Team's plan for the Sprint.
E. It is ordered by the Product Owner.

QUESTION 82

Sprint burndown charts are an efficient tracking tool, because they show:

A. An estimate of the total work remaining for the Sprint.
B. How much effort has gone into a Sprint.
C. How many hours have been worked by each Development Team member.
D. How many Product Backlog items remain.

QUESTION 83

A member of the Development Team takes the Scrum Master aside to express his concerns about data security issues. What should the Scrum Master do?

A. Add security to the definition of "Done".
B. Tell the Product Owner to stop further development of features until the issues are fixed.
C. Create a Product Backlog item for security.
D. Go check with the testers.
E. Ask the person to share the issue with the team as soon as possible.

QUESTION 84

The Product Backlog is ordered by:

A. The Product Owner with the most valuable items placed at the top.
B. Risk, where safer items are at the top, and riskier items are at the bottom.
C. Items are randomly arranged.
D. Size, where small items are at the top and large items are at the bottom.

QUESTION 85

What happens if the Development Team cannot complete its work by the end of the Sprint?

A. The Sprint is extended and future Sprints use this new duration.
B. The Sprint length holds and the Development Team continuously learns what is actually possible to do within a Sprint of this length.
C. The Sprint is extended temporarily. Lessons are taken to ensure it doesn't happen again.

QUESTION 86

User documentation is part of your definition of "Done". However, there aren't enough technical writers for all teams. Your Development Team doesn't have a technical writer. What should you do?

A. Form a separate team of technical writers that will work on an on-demand basis for the various Product Owners. Work order will be first in, first out.
B. Let the user documentation remain undone and accumulate until after the last development Sprint. It will then be done by any available technical writers.
C. Wait until you have a technical writer on your Development Team to take care of this.
D. Your Development Team is still responsible for creating user documentation. In this case, the Development Team members will write it.

QUESTION 87

You are the Scrum Master for four Scrum Teams working from the same Product Backlog. Several of the developers come to you complaining that work identified for the upcoming two Sprints will require full-time commitment from a technical specialist who is external to the teams. What are two key concerns for the Scrum Master to take into account in this situation? (Choose two.)

A. The desire to maintain a stable velocity.
B. The benefit of Development Teams figuring out a solution for themselves.
C. The need to have enough work to keep all Development Team members busy.
D. The ability of the Scrum Teams to produce integrated Increments.

QUESTION 88

A Scrum Team has been working on a product for nine Sprints. A new Product Owner comes in, understanding he is accountable for the Product Backlog. However, he is unsure about his responsibilities. Which two activities are part of the Product Owner role according to Scrum? (Choose two.)

A. Ensuring that the most valuable functionality is produced first, at all times.
B. Interacting with stakeholders.
C. Providing the Development Team with detailed specifications.
D. Describing features as Use Cases.
E. Creating detailed functional test cases.

QUESTION 89

What activities would a Product Owner typically undertake in the phase between the end of the current Sprint and the start of the next Sprint?

A. There are no such activities. The next Sprint starts immediately after the current Sprint.
B. Refine the Product Backlog.
C. Work with the Quality Assurance departments on the Increment of the current Sprint.
D. Update the project plan with stakeholders.

QUESTION 90

Why is the Daily Scrum held at the same time and same place?

A. The consistency reduces complexity.
B. The place can be named.
C. The Product Owner demands it.
D. Rooms are hard to book and this lets it be booked in advance.

QUESTION 91

Why does a Development Team need a Sprint Goal?

A. A Sprint Goal only gives purpose to Sprint 0.
B. Sprint Goals are not valuable. Everything is known from the Product Backlog.
C. The Development Team is more focused with a common yet specific goal.
D. A Sprint Goal ensures that all of the Product Backlog items selected for the Sprint are implemented.

QUESTION 92

When does the next Sprint begin?

A. When the Product Owner is ready.
B. Immediately after the conclusion of the previous Sprint.
C. The Monday following the Sprint Review.
D. Immediately following the next Sprint Planning.

QUESTION 93

Who should know the most about the progress toward a business objective or a release?

A. The Project Manager.
B. The Scrum Master.
C. The Development Team.
D. The Product Owner.

QUESTION 94

What are two ways that architecture and infrastructure are handled in Scrum? (Choose two.)

A. They are discussed, determined, and documented before the actual feature development Sprints.
B. They are implemented along with functional development of the product.
C. They are added to the Product Backlog and addressed in early Sprints, while always requiring at least some business functionality, no matter how small.
D. They are built by a separate team through the creation of an architectural runway.

QUESTION 95

What is the accountability of the Product Owner during Sprint 0?
(Choose the best answer.)

A. There is no such thing as Sprint 0.
B. Gathering, eliciting, and analyzing the requirements that will be inserted into the Product Backlog.
C. Make the complete project plan to commit date, budget, and scope to the stakeholders.
D. Determine the composition of the Development Teams so they have the capacity to deliver the completed forecast.
E. Make sure enough Product Backlog items are refined to fill the first 3 Sprints.

QUESTION 96

At the seventh Sprint Review, the stakeholders are disappointed and angry. They have determined that the product or system being built will not meet their needs and will cost more than they are willing to spend. What factors likely led to this? (Choose two.)

A. The Project Management Office (PMO) has not been engaged adequately.
B. The Product Owner has not been keeping the stakeholders aware of the progress of the project.
C. The stakeholders haven't been using the Sprint Reviews to inspect and evaluate progress.
D. The stakeholders were not allowed to enter the development area.

QUESTION 97

Every Scrum Team must have a Product Owner and Scrum Master. (Choose the best answer.)

A. True. Outcomes affected by their participation and availability.
B. False. A Product Owner can be replaced by a subject matter expert in the Scrum Team.
C. False. A Scrum Master is only required when asked for by the Scrum Team.
D. True. Each must be 100% dedicated to the Scrum Team.

QUESTION 98

Several Sprints into a project, the Product Owner tells the Scrum Master that a key stakeholder just started using the product. The stakeholder is unhappy with the quality of the product. What are two good options for the Scrum Master? (Choose the best two answers.)

A. Wait to bring this up until the Sprint Retrospective.
B. Encourage the Product Owner to put quality specifications on the Product Backlog and express the stakeholder's concern to the Developers.
C. Bring the concern to the testers to improve how the Product is verified.
D. Explain to the Product Owner that it is up to the Developers to decide on acceptable quality standards.
E. Coach the Product Owner on how to talk with the Developers about this concern.

QUESTION 99

Which of the following is a Developer accountable for? (Choose the best two answers.)

A. Selecting the Product Owner.
B. Reporting productivity.
C. Creating a plan for the Sprint, the Sprint Backlog.
D. Organizing the work required to meet the Sprint Goal.

QUESTION 100

What is the recommended size for a Scrum Team? (Choose the best answer.)

A. At least 7.
B. 9
C. 10 or fewer.
D. 7 plus or minus 3.

QUESTION 101

When must a Product Owner release each Increment? (Choose the best answer.)

A. When it makes sense.
B. When the Scrum Team finishes their work.
C. Whenever the product is free of defects.
D. After every Sprint, Without exception.

QUESTION 102

What techniques could the Scrum Master use when the Scrum Team gets caught in an internal disagreement about which agile practices to apply? (Choose the best two answers.)

A. Involve the complete Scrum Team in making a decision.
B. Use coaching techniques; such as open questions and active listening.
C. Ask an external agile coach what they recommend.
D. Ask team members to take the issue up with to the company's Human Resources department.

QUESTION 103
Which of the following is an example of an Increment? (Choose the best answer.)

A. A plan for the overall product release.
B. A mock-up of the product marketing materials.
C. A design for the product.
D. A product roll-out plan.
E. A valuable, useful set of products featured.
F. All of the above.

QUESTION 104
During the Sprint Retrospective a Scrum Team has identified several high priority process improvements. Which of the following statements is most accurate? (Choose the best answer.)

A. The Scrum Team may add items to the Sprint Backlog for the next Sprint.
B. The Scrum Team should choose at least one high priority process improvement to place in the Product Backlog.
C. The Scrum Team should decline to add a process improvement to the Sprint Backlog when things are running smoothly.
D. The Scrum Master selects the most important process improvement and places it in the Sprint Backlog

QUESTION 105
Which three of the following are true about Scrum? (Choose the best three answers.)

A. Scrum implements self-management by replacing Project Managers with Scrum Masters.
B. Each component of Scrum serves a specific purpose and is essential to Scrum's success and your usage of Scrum to develop complex products.
C. Scrum is a methodology where you can pick and choose which parts of Scrum you think will work for your environment.
D. Scrum is a framework for developing and sustaining complex products.
E. Scrum is based on empiricism and lean thinking.

QUESTION 106

Who is accountable for tracking the remaining work toward the Sprint Goal? (Choose the best answer.)

A. The Developers.
B. The Scrum Master.
C. The Product Owner.
D. The Project Manager.

QUESTION 107
Who is accountable for clearly expressing Product Backlog items? (Choose the best answer.)

A. The business analyst who represents the Product Owner.
B. The Product Owner.
C. The Scrum Master, or the Scrum Master may have the Developers do it.
D. The Scrum Master.

QUESTION 108
Which three of the following are time-boxed events in Scrum? (Choose the best three answers.)

A. Release Planning.
B. Release Retrospective.
C. Sprint Retrospective.
D. Sprint Planning.
E. Sprint Testing.
F. Sprint 0.
G. Daily Scrum.

ANSWERS

1. Correct Answer: B
2. Correct Answer: B
3. Correct Answer: C
4. Correct Answer: B
5. Correct Answer: C
6. Correct Answer: A
7. Correct Answer: C
8. Correct Answer: CE
9. Correct Answer: BDE
10. Correct Answer: B
11. Correct Answer: A
12. Correct Answer: A
13. Correct Answer: B
14. Correct Answer: BD
15. Correct Answer: B
16. Correct Answer: C
17. Correct Answer: A
18. Correct Answer: B
19. Correct Answer: A
20. Correct Answer: D
21. Correct Answer: D
22. Correct Answer: B
23. Correct Answer: CDF
24. Correct Answer: BC
25. Correct Answer: C
26. Correct Answer: B
27. Correct Answer: BE
28. Correct Answer: C
29. Correct Answer: A
30. Correct Answer: A
31. Correct Answer: D
32. Correct Answer: A

33. Correct Answer: A
34. Correct Answer: CD
35. Correct Answer: A
36. Correct Answer: B
37. Correct Answer: B
38. Correct Answer: B
39. Correct Answer: ABD
40. Correct Answer: B
41. Correct Answer: B
42. Correct Answer: A
43. Correct Answer: C
44. Correct Answer: C
45. Correct Answer: C
46. Correct Answer: B
47. Correct Answer: A
48. Correct Answer: ACE
49. Correct Answer: B
50. Correct Answer: D
51. Correct Answer: BC
52. Correct Answer: B
53. Correct Answer: A
54. Correct Answer: C
55. Correct Answer: A
56. Correct Answer: E
57. Correct Answer: BD
58. Correct Answer: C
59. Correct Answer: A
60. Correct Answer: B
61. Correct Answer: D
62. Correct Answer: D
63. Correct Answer: B
64. Correct Answer: A
65. Correct Answer: B
66. Correct Answer: A
67. Correct Answer: B
68. Correct Answer: BC
69. Correct Answer: A

70. Correct Answer: D

71. Correct Answer: AB

72. Correct Answer: C

73. Correct Answer: E

74. Correct Answer: B

75. Correct Answer: A

76. Correct Answer: C

77. Correct Answer: BD

78. Correct Answer: C

79. Correct Answer: E

80. Correct Answer: D

81. Correct Answer: A

82. Correct Answer: A

83. Correct Answer: E

84. Correct Answer: A

85. Correct Answer: B

86. Correct Answer: D

87. Correct Answer: BD

88. Correct Answer: AB

89. Correct Answer: A

90. Correct Answer: A

91. Correct Answer: C

92. Correct Answer: B

93. Correct Answer: D

94. Correct Answer: BC

95. Correct Answer: A

96. Correct Answer: AB

97. Correct Answer: A

98. Correct Answer: BC

99. Correct Answer: CD

100. Correct Answer: C

101. Correct Answer: A

102. Correct Answer: AB

103. Correct Answer: F

104. Correct Answer: A

105. Correct Answer: BDE

106. Correct Answer: A

107.   Correct Answer: B
108.   Correct Answer: CDG